THE WATERGATE SCANDAL

The conspiracy that brought down Nixon

Written by Quentin Convard
In collaboration with Pierre Frankignoulle
Translated by Jessica Foster

THE WATERGATE SCANDAL

KEY INFORMATION

- **When:** from 17 June 1972 to 9 August 1974.
- **Where:** Washington, D.C.
- **Context:** Richard Nixon's reelection.
- **People involved:**
  - Richard Nixon, American president (1913-1994).
  - Sam Ervin, American politician (1896-1985).
- **Impact:**
  - Crisis of confidence of the American general public regarding the president and his administration.
  - Nixon's replacement in the White House by Gerald Ford (1913-2006).

INTRODUCTION

How did a seemingly ordinary burglary lead to the resignation of the President of the United States two years later? The Watergate scandal, which resembled something between a detective novel and a legal battle, was followed by the resignation of many senior officials between 1972 and 1974, with the paranoid and omnipotent madness of the Nixon administration in the crosshairs. Additionally, it showed that American democracy was built on safeguards and a free press, avoiding the excesses that a president who was greedy for power and control could cause.

For the United States, the Watergate scandal was one of the major events of the second half of the 20th century.

Coinciding with the end of the Vietnam War (1954-1975) and the economic crisis that had appeared on the horizon, this scandal marked the end of an era and plunged the United States into a period of uncertainty.

CONTEXT

THE PRESIDENTIAL ELECTION

In 1972, the incumbent president Richard Nixon was facing the Democrat George McGovern (1922-2012) in the presidential election. Nixon had been elected in 1968 and could boast of having calmed the tense relations with the Soviet Union, boosted the economy and sent astronauts to the moon. But, above all, he was obsessed with security and control. Thus, during his first term as president, he removed all responsibility from his Cabinet in order to better concentrate the power in the hands of a few collaborators whom he trusted completely, such as Henry Kissinger (born in 1923), John Ehrlichman (1925-1999) and H. R. Haldeman (1926-1993). Haldeman, who had previously worked in advertising, helped the Californian to transform the White House into a permanent communication tool by using information and controlling his image, which the president was obsessed with.

Up against the incumbent president was the Democratic Senator from South Dakota, George McGovern, a fierce opponent of the Vietnam War. He advocated the establishment of a minimum wage and supported improving relations with Fidel Castro (Cuban head of state, 1926-2016). Considered too left wing, the Democrats' candidate was not particularly eminent and, moreover, only owed his nomination to the withdrawal of the party's two leading figures, Edmund Muskie (1914-1996), the Senator for Maine, and Ted Kennedy (1932-2009). The former was the victim of a conspiracy orchestrated by the Republican Party, which sent a letter in which Muskie badmouthed French Canadians to the media. The letter later turned out to be fake, but his reputation would never recover from it. Ted Kennedy, on the other hand, quit the race in 1969, following the Chappaquiddick incident, for which he was responsible and which caused the death of his companion, Mary Jo Kopechne. Consequently, for Nixon, the election was nothing more than a formality.

AN AIR OF CONTESTATION

The early 1970s were marked by various protest movements in the United States. The Black Panther Party (an African-American revolutionary movement) and the Weather Underground (an American anti-racism and anti-capitalism collective), to name just two, sent shockwaves across the American white middle classes, causing fear that added to that already provoked by the race riots of the late 1960s, thus destroying all the progress made by President Lyndon B. Johnson (1908-1973) regarding civil rights. What had been a central question in the 1960s became secondary after the assassination of the pacifist leader Martin Luther King (1929-1968) on 4 April 1968, a period during which violent groups appeared. While the Americans did not experience chaos on the same level as the events in France in May 1968, everyone still felt and believed that society should evolve towards greater equality and that it should focus on its internal problems, notably by pulling out of the stalemate that was the Vietnam War.

During the 1968 elections, the Vietnam War was thus at the

heart of nearly all the debates. With Johnson's leadership widely criticised, Nixon had no choice but to promise to rapidly withdraw troops from the war, while maintaining America's honour, to win over the electorate. While he began to withdraw troops as soon as he was elected, paradoxically, the bombardments intensified. Additionally, the United States invaded Cambodia on 29 April 1970 without the prior agreement of Congress. Many anti-war student protests subsequently broke out across the country. Some were violently repressed, but all of them illustrated the absolute will of the people to put an end to the war, even more so after the Pentagon Papers.

THE PENTAGON PAPERS

On 30 June 1971, the Supreme Court cleared the *New York Times* and the *Washington Post* for publishing a secret investigation into the United States' involvement in Vietnam, ordered by the Defense Secretary Robert McNamara (American politician, 1916-2009). This 7000-page report, which was leaked to the press by the military analyst Daniel Ellsberg (born in 1931) at the start of 1971 and proved that the government had deliberately intensified the war via secret operations, scandalised the general public and eventually persuaded the Americans to end the Vietnam War. While it was mainly John F. Kennedy and Lyndon B. Johnson who were discredited by the Pentagon Papers, Nixon was furious that his files had been leaked and saw the Supreme Court's decision as an affront to the government. This incident reinforced his belief that the liberal press of the East Coast was a major enemy of his administration.

THE POWER OF THE *WASHINGTON POST*

From the moment he entered the White House, Nixon privately gave 'black marks' to journalists who were too critical for his liking, and regarded the intellectual press of the East Coast cities with suspicion. And for good reason: Watergate would be mostly uncovered and investigated by the *Washington Post*.

After the Second World War, the press changed dramatically in the United States. Many magazines and newspapers disappeared and each city had at most two or three different newspapers, often owned by the same person. Washington had two daily papers: the *Post* in the morning and the *Star*, which went on sale in the evening. The former, following a merger with the *Times Herald* under the Kennedy administration, became one of the country's most influential publications. When its owner Phil Graham (1915-1963) died, his wife Katharine (1917-2001) became its sole commander-in-chief, and increased the paper's financial revenue by acquiring a weekly magazine, a television channel and a radio station, among other things. With 530 000 copies printed during the week, and 720 000 at the weekend, the *Post*, due to its financial empire and its geographical location, became a point of reference for the media world. Independent and liberal-leaning, the newspaper had a team of experienced writers led by the editor Ben Bradlee (1921-2014).

The newspapers played an essential role in American democracy, as freedom of speech and of the press were inscribed in the First Amendment to the Constitution. Thus, in a country with no national daily press, local publications competed and were always on the lookout for any potential scandal, paying particular attention to any wrongdoing by those in power.

BIOGRAPHIES

RICHARD NIXON, AMERICAN HEAD OF STATE

Portrait of Richard Nixon.

The son of a storeowner, Nixon was inaugurated as the

37th president of the United States on 20 January 1969, succeeding Lyndon B. Johnson. Before he won this election, the Californian had been a Member of the US House of Representatives from California's 12th district from 1950 until 1953. He was then chosen by the Republican Party to be Eisenhower's (1890-1969) running mate in the 1952 presidential elections, and thus became his vice president from 1953 until 1961.

In May 1960, he ran for the Republican nomination, but narrowly lost out to John F. Kennedy. He ran again success-fully in 1968 when, by centring his campaign on the rees-tablishment of law and order, he defeated the Democrats' candidate Hubert Humphrey (1911-1978). These elections were very unusual in that a third-party candidate made it to the final run-off. The Democratic Governor of Alabama, George Wallace (1919-1998), won 13.5% of the vote and 46 seats in the Electoral College.

After his reelection in 1972, Nixon's term was marked by the Vietnam War, the beginning of the détente with the Soviet bloc and astronauts Neil Armstrong and Buzz Aldrin's moon landing on 21 July 1969, a formative moment for the Americans which overrode the disappointment experienced in 1957 when the USSR had successfully launched its first Sputnik into orbit. Nixon's second term met an abrupt end with the Watergate scandal, which forced him to resign on 9 August 1974.

After being pardoned by President Gerald Ford, Nixon resumed an ordinary life. Recognising that he had made a blunder, he published his memoirs in 1978. From then on, the 37th US president's life oscillated between that of an outcast, a well-known and sought-after speaker and a politician who was liked by various foreign heads of state, such as Deng Xiaoping (Chinese statesmen, 1904-1997).

On 18 April 1994, Nixon suffered a heart attack and died four days later.

SAM ERVIN, AMERICAN POLITICIAN

Portrait of Sam Ervin.

Ervin was from North Carolina and was the state's Senator
from 1954 to 1974. A hero of the First World War (1914-1918),
during which he fought in France, he graduated with a law
degree from Harvard in 1922. He was elected Representative

of Burke County in 1922, 1924 and 1930.

His time as senator was marked by his opposition to civil rights legislation, which led him to pronounce himself against the Supreme Court's decision to repeal racial segregation in public schools in 1956. Nominated by the Democrats to preside over the investigation committee for the Watergate scandal, he resigned in December 1974, shortly before the end of his term. He then resumed his career as a jurist and became an advisor to a law firm.

He died of an illness at the age of 88.

THE WATERGATE SCANDAL

THE WHITE HOUSE PLUMBERS

The Watergate scandal began on 17 June 1972, when the DNC headquarters were broken into. While the presence of five burglars in the prestigious Watergate complex did not shock the police, their profile, on the other hand, turned out to be unusual, and the questioning that followed only added to the confusion.

Aerial view of the Watergate building, photograph taken in 2006.

The crooks were arrested with all the equipment of spies in training: rubber gloves, cameras, walkie-talkies and electronic equipment necessary for wiretapping were all retrieved as evidence. Four of the suspects were from Cuba and the fifth, James McCord (born in 1924), belonged to the Committee for the Re-Election of the President (CRP), an organisation established by Nixon's allies for the 1972 presidential election. Even more surprisingly, McCord was also a former CIA and FBI agent, as well as a lieutenant colonel in the US Air Force Reserve. Additionally, the agents who carried out the investigation found a hotel room key in the possession of the Plumbers (a nickname given to them retrospectively, because they were the ones who had to stop the leaks) and, in the hotel room, a significant sum of money, as well as a notebook featuring the name of Howard Hunt (1918-2007), an American spy and author who was involved with the White House. What at first seemed like an ordinary burglary turned out to be a story worthy of a great detective novel. As Washington is a federal district, the FBI led the inquiry.

As the days went by, everything seemed to point to the CRP and the White House. On 28 June 1972, a dramatic turn of events occurred: G. Gordon Liddy (born in 1930) resigned from his position on the CRP after refusing to answer the FBI agents' questions, leading them to suspect that he was linked with the affair. On 8 July, John N. Mitchell (1913-1988), a former attorney general, stood down as head of the Committee. The investigators and the general public were left confused. Why had the Plumbers broken into the DNC headquarters? To wiretap it? Who was in charge of the operation? How much of the responsibility lay with the CRP and its leaders? Nixon, for his part, denied any White House involvement.

Without the tireless work of the *Washington Post* and its two journalists Carl Bernstein (born in 1944) and Bob Woodward (born in 1943), the break-in at Watergate would certainly have remained an unclear affair, categorised as normal politician behaviour. But the two reporters persevered, and their determination eventually paid off. Helped by a secret informant, nicknamed Deep Throat, they unearthed information about the illegal funding of the CRP, whose money paid for the burglars' defence. They also discovered that Donald Segretti (born in 1941), who was part of the same committee, had been tasked with destroying the Democrats' campaign by stretching his ingenuity to defame the leaders of the opposition party. Bernstein and Woodward's work showcased the disloyal manipulations of the Republican Party in the presidential campaign, as well as the link between the burglars and the key figures in the CRP, Hunt and Liddy, who had planned everything. It was not until 2005 that Deep Throat revealed his identity: the mysterious informant was none other than Mark Felt (1913-2008), the Associate Director of the FBI at the time the events happened.

While the *Washington Post* did not uncover everything, the results of its investigation were corroborated and completed by the FBI's detailed inquiry and the many witnesses who were called to the stand before a jury, which would allow light to be cast over some of the less clear facts. Throughout the affair, the press played its role of bridging the knowledge gap between the investigators and the general public perfectly, keeping the public informed and ensuring that the burglary was not quickly forgotten. Thus, faced with the evidence mounting against them, the perpetrators of the break-in were frightened and began to speak. The time for confessions had arrived.

THE TIME OF REVELATIONS

Although the Republican Party's methods were discredited, the affair had not yet tarnished Nixon's reputation, and he was elected with a clear majority (61% of the votes) over the Democrat George McGovern. Congress did not have a Republican majority, however, which showed that in the early 1970s the United States was more pro-Nixon than truly Republican.

Nixon got carried away with his reelection and thought that Watergate would be forgotten and overshadowed by his victory. But on 8 January 1973, the trial of the seven charged suspects began, presided over by Judge John Sirica (1904-1992), who was known for his severity. Hunt and the four American-Cubans pleaded guilty, avoiding trial by jury. McCord and Liddy therefore found themselves alone before the court. While the latter was almost silent throughout the trial, the former was much more forthcoming with information. He admitted that he had been pressured to stay silent and confirmed that the president's legal advisor, John W. Dean (born in 1938), had known about the Watergate operation.

The trial ended on 2 February, and the sentence would be pronounced on 23 March. In the meantime, however,

Congress got involved in the matter and tasked the North Carolina Senator, Sam Ervin, with leading a special commission of inquiry into the presidential campaign.

COMMISSIONS OF INQUIRY

Congress can establish commissions of inquiry for anything and can call witnesses during them. If they lie, they are charged with perjury. These commissions are not courts: consequently, they can neither judge nor sentence. However, they still carry a certain weight and, in the past, have enabled gangster networks to be disbanded.

At the same time, Nixon had to appoint a new FBI director following the death of J. Edgar Hoover (1885-1972). Patrick Gray (1916-2005) was chosen, but he had to be approved by the Senate before taking up the position. The Senate took advantage of this to ask him some questions, and thus learned that the White House had demanded that an FBI agent, John W. Dean, monitor the federal agents' investigation and that, additionally, he may have lied about certain things. Gray did not come out of these revelations well and Nixon withdrew his support for him. At around the same time, the general public learned of the existence of this special team, nicknamed the White House Plumbers, which had been established by Hunt and Liddy, who had already been used prior to Watergate. It was discovered that they had ransacked the office of Lewis Fielding, who was the psychiatrist of Daniel Ellsberg, who had released the Pentagon

Papers. Following these revelations, rumours went around that John W. Dean was going to resign, but he refused to become the scapegoat for the affair.

By April 1973, there was no longer any doubt that the White House was involved in the scandal, the only unclear part was to what extent – and that was another story entirely. Feeling the noose tightening around him, Nixon was forced to react to try to clear himself of suspicion. On 30 April, he announced the resignation of John W. Dean (whom he had fired) and his two closest collaborators, John Ehrlichman and H. R. Haldeman. In doing so, Nixon tried to clear his name by passing blame onto these three men.

NIXON'S RECORDINGS

Ervin's commission began its work on 17 May 1973. The very next day, Elliot L. Richardson (1920-1999), the new Attorney General, appointed Archibald Cox (1912-2004), a Harvard law professor and former third-in-command in the Department of Justice under the Kennedy administration, to the position of Solicitor General.

The debates were broadcast on television. While the witnesses, mostly unknown to the general public, flocked to the commission, the first main event was John W. Dean's statement, on 25 June 1973. He mentioned various wrongdoings committed by the Republicans and even directly incriminated President Nixon, as well as his special advisor, Charles Colson (1931-2012). However, he did not present many documents and his statement was considered to be that of a bitter former collaborator. Nixon was given a moment of respite, but it would be short-lived.

On 13 July 1973, Alexander Butterfield (born in 1926) came to the stand. He was Haldeman's former deputy, and revealed, in the course of his questioning, that Nixon had recorded all his interviews without his interlocutors' knowledge, which astounded the commission and the general public. These revelations harmed the president's popularity, which was in freefall in the polls. His press conferences also became much more tense.

The commission, meanwhile, demanded the tapes from the White House, to see if Nixon knew about the CRP's actions. But the president refused to hand them over, arguing that the executive body had no obligations towards the legislative body where confidential documents were concerned. Cox and Ervin thus took advantage of the courts. Sirica forced the White House to hand over the tapes on 19 October 1973. The president then proposed a deal: if the judge accepted the transcriptions of the recordings instead of the recordings themselves, he would not call upon the Supreme Court.

Nixon forced to hand over the transcripts of the tapes.

THE SATURDAY NIGHT MASSACRE

Cox refused to accept the compromise proposed by the president and told him this on Saturday 20 October during a press conference. Nixon was furious and asked Elliot L. Richardson to dismiss the special prosecutor. He refused and resigned in the process to reinforce his point. The president then turned to Richardson's second-in-command, William Ruckelshaus (born in 1932), who refused and also resigned from his post. The president then asked Robert Bork (1927-2012), the third-in-command in the Department of Justice, who accepted and dismissed Cox.

The media jumped on this event, nicknaming it the 'Saturday Night Massacre', inciting anger among the population, who did not agree with this show of force from the executive branch. The tapes were at the heart of the scandal and there was no doubt that all the necessary answers were on them. In the eyes of the general public, Nixon was now a tyrant.

At the same time, Vice President Spiro Agnew (1918-1996) resigned from his post for somewhat undignified reasons. When he was Governor of Maryland, he had reportedly accepted bribes from companies for public works. This matter, revealed by the *Wall Street Journal*, became increasingly significant, up to the point at which it forced him to resign. Nixon saw this as his opportunity to distract the public, but in vain: for Americans, the entire Nixon administration was corrupt. Agnew's resignation would simply be a prelude to Nixon's inevitable downfall.

NIXON'S DOWNFALL

Following the Saturday Night Massacre, 84 members of the House of Representatives signed an impeachment motion which was then sent to the Judiciary Committee, overseen by the Democrat Peter W. Rodino (1909-2005). The committee, which received one million dollars for the investigation, was made up of many experts and lawyers, and brought six charges relative to Nixon's term:

- the break-in at Watergate and the funding of the suspects' lawyers;
- the 1972 electoral campaign and the abuses committed by the Republican Party;
- the surveillance by the White House Plumbers;

- the president's funding – he was believed to have embezzled ten million dollars to fund his secondary residences;
- the use of state agencies to serve his campaign's generous donors;
- the bombing of Cambodia (1969-1973), which happened without the prior agreement of Congress, as well as the illegal dismantling of the Office of Economic Opportunity.

IMPEACHMENTS

This procedure, which originates from the United Kingdom, enables judicial proceedings to be brought against top officials. Only the House of Representatives has the power to impeach. If the president is the one being judged, the Chief Justice leads the debate. The sentence must be passed with a two-thirds majority. It leads to the deposition of the person who is found guilty, but not a criminal conviction. There is no jury during an impeachment process.

With the exception of the sixth accusation, the tapes were at the heart of the debate. Nixon handed the nine promised tapes over to the new special prosecutor, Leon Jaworski (1905-1982). But of the nine conversations, two had not been recorded. Additionally, 18 minutes had been manually erased from the conversation that had taken place on 20 June 1972, which was the most important one of all. While the president's personal secretary took the fall for the destruction of the tapes, no one believed this, and the press blamed a desperate attempt by Nixon to hide the truth.

On 30 April 1974, Nixon tried a new tactic to get himself out of the scandal. He appeared on television and announced that the White House had transcribed all 46 conversations about Watergate. This was supposed to be a diversion, but turned out to be a very bad idea. As the tapes' transcription was done in haste, some parts were deliberately left out, while others showed a less stellar side to Nixon's personality, which harmed his popularity even more.

Demonstrators march in favour of Nixon's impeachment.

On 24 July 1974, the Supreme Court ruled in favour of the commission of inquiry. As four of its members had been appointed by Nixon himself, one might have expected some indulgence towards the president on the part of Chief Justice Warren Burger and his deputies, but this was not the case. On 5 August 1974, the White House handed over the tapes containing the conversations that had taken place on 23 June 1972 between Nixon and Haldeman. It was then clear that the president had done all he could to halt the FBI inquiry. Driven into a corner, on 8 August 1974, he announced that he would step down the next day. On 9 August, Vice President Gerald Ford was sworn in and became the 38th President of the United States.

Portrait of Gerald Ford.

IMPACT

PRESIDENTIAL PARDON

Nixon's resignation brought the arrival of a new White House resident, Gerald Ford, who soon had to rule on the penalty for his predecessor. On 8 September 1974, he made a very unpopular decision. While the general public believed that Nixon should appear in court, the new president decided to pardon him, which ended all legal proceedings. In return, he asked Nixon to write a text apologising and recognising his wrongdoings. Although he refused, Ford still decided to pardon him, despite everything.

A NEW PERCEPTION OF POLITICS

The Watergate scandal changed the way that Americans understood politics. Coupled with the end of the Vietnam War and the financial crisis, this affair profoundly altered America, making it a more individualist country, and one that was riddled with uncertainties.

However, no noteworthy changes were visible in politics. The two-party system remained the prevailing model, despite the population's increasing suspicion towards the Democrats and the Republicans, who were incapable of finding new ideas to modernise the country and were now perceived as electoral machines with no substance or consistency. To find new ideas, the population would have to look to the smaller parties, of which there were many at the time. But although Americans saw a certain appeal in those parties, they still did not vote for them.

This period also saw the bolstering of pressure groups and lobbyists. Whether they were religious, ethnic, professional, geographical or ideological, these associations successfully met with general approval due to the homogeneity of their members and the idea of the common good that motivated them. Thus, regions or states opposed them in order to defend their interests. This antagonism could also be found within single states, where communities fought one another.

The lack of trust in the political class accelerated this process, which divided the country and launched it into a logic of vested interests, which the Secretary of Energy under Jimmy Carter (born in 1924), James R. Schlesinger (1929-2014), denounced as the 'balkanisation' of the United States.

POLITICAL UPSET

For 40 years, the power of the American president had been increasing, to the detriment of Congress. The presidency had now almost become an absolute monarchy – a terrible affront to a country that swore by democracy and mistrusted federal power. While Nixon seemed to have gone further than his predecessors, this was maybe just because his embezzlement had been discovered and he had often thought that he was justified in bypassing laws and the Constitution by virtue of the power he had.

Nixon's wrongdoings therefore ended this era of all-powerful presidency. After the scandal, the White House lost its splendour in the eyes and hearts of Americans and was now last place in a list of 22 institutions: in the late 1970s, only 18% of the population stated that they trusted the government.

Congress therefore tried to get the situation under control. In 1973, it passed the War Powers Resolution, a law that limited the president's power in military interventions. It also bolstered its budgetary control: from now on, the president could no longer impound appropriated funds, as Nixon had done with the Office of Economic Opportunity. In 1971, a law was also passed aimed at restricting the financial abuses committed in the previous elections. Various amendments would complement this text throughout the decade. However, Congress became no more powerful, and the creation of more sub-committees, which led to duplications, led inexperienced legislators to rule in chaotic and complicated conditions.

We might imagine that the Watergate scandal would renew liberal ideas insofar as it disgraced Nixon, who was at the peak of his conservative politics. In the long term, however, this was not the case. The Democrats certainly made significant gains in Congress in the 1974 elections, and in 1976, the Governor of Georgia, Jimmy Carter, was elected president; however, this only lasted four years. Ronald Reagan (1911-2004), a champion of ultra-conservatism, would win in the 1980s. This former film actor personified the changes happening within the Republican Party. Moderate Republicans were soon overwhelmed by new conservative figures, such as George H. W. Bush (born in 1924), Donald Rumsfeld (born in 1932) and Dick Cheney (born in 1941).

MONICAGATE

The Watergate scandal convinced the public that the worst offence a president could commit was lying. The image of an omnipotent president had changed to that of an irreproachable and virtuous president. Almost 30 years after Nixon's escapades, this idea was still firmly anchored in American culture. Thus, in 1998, the Democratic president Bill Clinton (born in 1946) was threatened with impeachment – although he was acquitted by the Senate – after lying under oath about the sexual relations he had with a White House intern, Monica Lewinsky (born in 1973).

SUMMARY

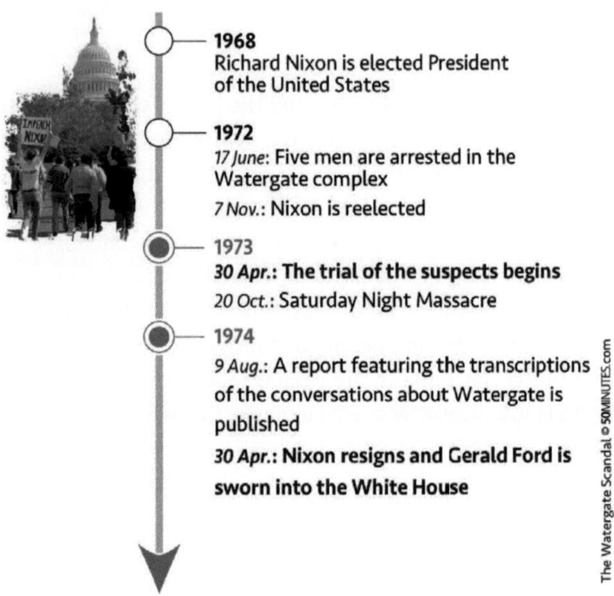

1968
Richard Nixon is elected President
of the United States

1972
17 June: Five men are arrested in the
Watergate complex
7 Nov.: Nixon is reelected

1973
***30 Apr.*: The trial of the suspects begins**
20 Oct.: Saturday Night Massacre

1974
9 Aug.: A report featuring the transcriptions
of the conversations about Watergate is
published
***30 Apr.*: Nixon resigns and Gerald Ford is
sworn into the White House**

- On 17 June 1972, the police arrested five people in the Watergate complex. The White House Plumbers, as they were known, seemed to be trained spies who had gone to place microphones in the DNC headquarters rather than ordinary burglars. Soon, the investigation led back to the Committee for the Re-Election of the President (CRP), as well as to Howard Hunt and G. Gordon Liddy, two prominent members of the CRP.
- The *Washington Post* revealed that the CRP had put a wide-scale spy network in place and that Watergate was

not its first activity.

- This did not affect the popularity of Richard Nixon, who was reelected president on 7 November 1972.
- On 30 April 1973, the trial of the suspects began, overseen by Judge Sirica. There it came to light that senior White House officials were involved in the Watergate break-in. Feeling the noose tighten around his neck, Nixon had three of his closest collaborators resign: John W. Dean, John Ehrlichman and H. R. Haldeman.
- On 16 July 1973, before Senator Ervin's commission, one of Haldeman's collaborators admitted that Nixon recorded all his conversations without his interlocutors' knowledge. Both the general public and the commission were appalled when they discovered this.
- Following an endless imbroglio concerning the president's tapes, which could have shed light on the matter, the special prosecutor Archibald Cox, Elliot L. Richardson and William Ruckelshaus were forced to step down from their posts. The newspapers soon nicknamed this evening of 20 October 1973 the 'Saturday Night Massacre'.
- The House of Representatives almost unanimously authorised the Judiciary Committee to start an impeachment process against Nixon.
- On 30 April 1974, the White House published a report featuring the transcriptions of Nixon's conversations, but this was not enough to appease the general public, nor Leon Jaworski, the new special prosecutor.
- As the months passed, Nixon became increasingly cornered and had no choice but to hand the tapes over and resign on 9 August 1974. His successor, Gerald Ford, however, decided to pardon him.

FIND OUT MORE

BIBLIOGRAPHY

- Aitken, J. (1996) *Nixon: A Life.* Washington: Regnery Publishing.
- Bernstein, C. and Woodward, B. (1974) *All the President's Men.* New York: Simon & Schuster.
- Coppolani, A. (2013) *Richard Nixon.* Paris: Fayard.
- Durandin, C. (2001) *Nixon, le président maudit.* Paris: Grancher.
- Kaspi, A. (1983) *Le Watergate.* Brussels: Éditions Complexe.
- Kaspi, A. (1986) *Les Américains : Les États- Unis de 1945 à nos jours.* Paris: Seuil.
- Kroes, C. (1974) *Watergate : série noire pour la Maison-Blanche.* Paris: Éditions Sociales.
- McCarthy, M. (1974) *Le Watergate : la tragédie de l'Amérique.* Paris: Gallimard.
- Mélandri, P. (2008) *Histoire des États- Unis : Le déclin ?.* Vol. 1. Paris: Perrin.
- Moisy, C. (1994) *Nixon et le Watergate : la chute d'un président.* Paris: Hachette.
- Zoller, E. (1999) *De Nixon à Clinton : malentendus juridiques transatlantiques.* Paris: Presses universitaires de France.

ICONOGRAPHIC SOURCES

- Portrait of Richard Nixon. Royalty-free reproduction picture.
- Portrait of Sam Ervin. Royalty-free reproduction picture.
- Aerial view of the Watergate building, photograph taken in 2006. Royalty-free reproduction picture.
- Nixon forced to hand over the transcripts of the tapes. Royalty-free reproduction picture.
- Demonstrators march in favour of Nixon's impeachment. Royalty-free reproduction picture.
- Portrait of Gerald Ford. Royalty-free reproduction picture.